It's another Quality Book from CGP

This book is for anyone doing GCSE English.

First we take all the really important stuff
you need to write good English
— and we stick it in a book.

Then we have a real good stab at trying
to make it funny — so you'll actually use it.

Simple as that.

What CGP is all about

Our sole aim here at CGP is to produce the highest quality
books — carefully written, immaculately presented, and
dangerously close to being funny.

Then we work our socks off to get them out to you
— at the cheapest possible prices.

Contents

SECTION FIVE — KINDS OF TEXT

SECTION SIX — WORDS ABOUT WRITING

SECTION SEVEN — POETRY

Published by Coordination Group Publications
Typesetting, and layout by The English Coordination Group

Written and co-edited by: Gemma Hallam BA (Hons)

Design, graphics and additional writing: Kate Stevens BSc (Hons)
Additional illustrations: Gemma Hallam, Ashley Tyson and Lex Ward

ISBN   1-84146-104-0

Groovy website: www.cgpbooks.co.uk

Jolly bits of clipart from CorelDRAW.

Printed by Elanders Hindson, Newcastle upon Tyne.

1101

Nouns and Pronouns

That's right — you've probably seen this before, but it really is <u>very important</u> to get it right. Make sure you learn this page <u>thoroughly</u>.

Nouns name things

A noun is a word that names a <u>thing</u>, like a <u>person</u>, an <u>animal</u> or a <u>place</u>. Remember — there are three kinds of noun that you need to know about.

<u>Proper</u> nouns are the names of particular people, places or things.

eg. Jane, Lancaster, Everest

<u>Common</u> nouns name kinds of thing.

eg. banana, dog, table

<u>Collective</u> nouns name groups of things.

eg. family, army, herd

Pronouns do the Job of Nouns

<u>Pronouns</u> are there so you don't have to <u>repeat</u> things over and over again.

<u>Charlie</u> picked up his bag and put <u>it</u> over his shoulder.

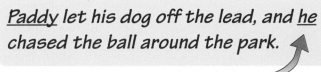

<u>Paddy</u> let his dog off the lead, and <u>he</u> chased the ball around the park.

Watch out! It isn't clear who you're talking about.

"Whose coat is that?" asked Tina.
"It's <u>mine</u>," Fleur replied.

'Mine' is a pronoun. It's used instead of writing 'Fleur's coat'.

Fleur wouldn't say 'Fleur's coat' herself. That'd be daft.

That's my coat!

"Hey!" shouted Fleur. "That's <u>my</u> coat!"

'My' is a pronoun as well. It's there instead of 'Fleur's'.

Me, my and mine — a mine of information...

The bit that needs <u>thinking</u> about is that words like "<u>mine</u>" and "<u>yours</u>" are <u>pronouns</u>, too. They go in place of <u>nouns</u>, you see. The rest of it should be fairly easy, I reckon.

Verbs

Verbs are something you've met <u>already</u>. The thing is, you need to know more about them now. Read on, and find out the <u>gory details</u>.

Verbs are Doing and Being words

Verbs are <u>action</u> or <u>being</u> words. They tell you what a person or thing is doing. Remember that <u>every single sentence</u> needs a <u>verb</u>. If it <u>hasn't</u> got a verb, it <u>isn't</u> a sentence.

Jodie <u>plays</u> football.

'Plays' is the verb.

Ben <u>is</u> the goalkeeper.

'Is' is the verb.

The Person of a Verb tells you Who

Things written from the point of view of 'I' are in the <u>first</u> person. Instructions written <u>to</u> someone are in the <u>second</u> person. Stories <u>about</u> someone are in the <u>third</u> person.

I am	first person	*we are*	first person (plural)
you are	second person	*you are*	second person (plural)
he is, she is, it is	third person	*they are*	third person (plural)

The Tense of a Verb tells you When

The <u>tense</u> of a verb can be <u>past</u>, <u>present</u> or <u>future</u>.
Some tenses need a <u>helping</u> verb.

Jodie <u>is playing</u> football.

The two words 'is playing' are a <u>verb phrase</u>. You need both words together to make this tense of the verb 'to play'.

'Is' is a helping verb.

This is going on right now.

Jodie <u>has been playing</u> football.

'Has' and 'been' are helping verbs.

This has been happening in the past.

Jodie <u>will go</u> ice-skating.

'Will' is a helping verb.

This will happen in the future.

Verbs

This page is all about <u>active</u> and <u>passive</u> verbs. Sounds complicated, but it just means there are <u>two ways</u> that you can talk about actions.

Active verbs tell you Who's Doing them

<u>Active</u> verbs make it <u>clear</u> who's doing the action. The sentence is <u>about</u> the person or thing <u>doing</u> the action. The <u>verb</u> goes with the noun or pronoun that <u>does</u> the action.

<u>Tricia</u> opened the <u>parcel</u>.

This is the person doing the action.

This is the thing that the action was done to.

<u>We</u> agree that fighting is wrong.

Passive verbs tell you What's Being Done

<u>Passive</u> verbs say what's happening, but they <u>don't</u> always say <u>who</u> or <u>what</u> is doing the action. The sentence is <u>about</u> the person or the thing that the action happens <u>to</u>.

This sentence doesn't tell you who opened the parcel.

The <u>parcel</u> was opened.

This is the thing that the action was done to.

It could have been opened by Sam, Priya, the Queen or a busload of aliens. We don't know.

Planet Travel

The parcel was opened <u>by</u> Tricia.

The word 'by' goes in front of the person or thing that did the action.

This sentence tells you the same information as 'Tricia opened the parcel'.

No Fighting

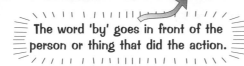
<u>It is</u> agreed that fighting is wrong.

This doesn't tell you who agreed that fighting is wrong.

Don't be passive — get up and get learning...

These two truly excellent pages on <u>verbs</u> go over some things you <u>already</u> know, and help you to get it fixed in that head of yours. Make sure you understand the <u>new stuff</u> about <u>active</u> and <u>passive</u> verbs. Take your <u>time</u> and go over it again and again until you've <u>got to grips</u> with it all.

4

The Imperative and Rhetorical Questions

It's useful to be able to <u>boss</u> people around, and this page tells you how to do it in style.

The <u>Imperative</u> Tells Someone to <u>Do</u> Something

The imperative is for <u>telling</u> someone to do something, or <u>asking</u> someone to do something.

The <u>verb</u> is at the <u>front</u>.

<u>Be</u> careful with that elephant!

It <u>doesn't</u> say, '<u>You</u> are careful with that elephant.'

Imperatives are often '<u>Don'ts</u>'.

<u>Don't</u> run in the corridor!

Put '<u>please</u>' on the <u>end</u> of the imperative to make it <u>polite</u>.

Pass me the custard <u>please</u>.

It <u>doesn't</u> say, '<u>You</u> pass me the custard.'

A <u>Rhetorical</u> <u>Question</u> <u>Isn't</u> a <u>Proper</u> <u>Question</u>

<u>Rhetorical</u> questions are questions that you <u>aren't</u> meant to give an <u>answer</u> to. The answer is so obvious that it doesn't need to be said.

Who would have thought the train would be late?

This is a joke — you don't want anyone to give an answer. You're really saying "I'm not surprised the train is late."

You use rhetorical questions to make really <u>strong statements</u> — especially if you're <u>arguing</u> or making a <u>speech</u>.

What time does the train arrive?

This is a real question — you do want an answer.

Was it ever more true to say we love our tea-bags?

This really means...

We love our tea bags!

Would you like to learn this? — so do it now...

A question that isn't <u>really</u> a question — that sounds a bit <u>deep</u>. Actually, you hear people asking <u>rhetorical questions</u> all the time. The main point to remember is that they <u>don't</u> expect an answer — they're just saying it for <u>effect</u> in a speech, or making a <u>strong statement</u>.

Adjectives and Adverbs

Here's a way of making your writing more <u>interesting</u>. Adjectives are for <u>describing</u> things and adverbs are the '-ly' words that say <u>how</u> something was <u>done</u>.

Adjectives are Describing Words

<u>Adjectives</u> describe <u>nouns</u> and tell you <u>more</u> about them.
Adjectives give you a <u>better picture</u> of the things that they describe.

The caterpillar wore <u>baggy</u> <u>pink</u> socks.

Not just any old socks, but baggy pink ones...

Baggy and pink are the <u>adjectives</u>.
They <u>describe</u> the socks.

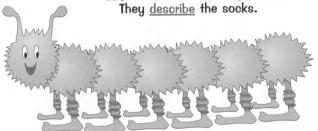

All his feet felt <u>cosy</u> and <u>warm</u>.

Cosy and warm are the <u>adjectives</u>.
This time, they <u>aren't</u> next to the word that they're describing.

Adverbs describe Verbs

Adverbs are often '-ly' words. They say <u>how</u> something was <u>done</u>.

Martin strolled home <u>slowly</u>.

He waved at us <u>in a friendly way</u>.

You can't say 'friendlily'. It's not a proper word.

Some <u>adjectives</u>, like 'lovely' and 'friendly' end in '-ly-' as well. Watch out with those — they <u>aren't adverbs</u>.

Adverbs describe Adjectives

Words like 'totally', 'quite' and 'very' are <u>adverbs</u>.
They're used with <u>adjectives</u> to show <u>how much</u> the adjective is working on the noun.

He was <u>very</u> old.

It was the best of pages, it was the worst...

Although these are words that you've come across before, they're pretty <u>important</u>.
<u>Adjectives</u> and <u>adverbs</u> give a <u>picture</u> of what you're writing about. <u>Without</u> them, writing would be more <u>boring</u> than <u>six weeks</u> counting sheep on a cold, damp Cumbrian hillside.

Prepositions

Prepositions show what's <u>under</u> what, who's <u>next to</u> who, what's <u>where</u> and what's <u>when</u>. My, that didn't sound in the <u>least</u> bit confusing... Read on, and all will be made clear.

Prepositions <u>say</u> Where things Are

<u>Prepositions</u> are words and phrases like '<u>under</u>', '<u>in front of</u>', '<u>between</u>' and '<u>with</u>'. They tell you the <u>relation</u> between nouns or pronouns.

Dennis sat <u>under</u> the weight.

Brian stepped <u>on</u> the sandwich.

Bob got <u>into</u> the sink.

There are plenty <u>more</u> prepositions out there. The <u>best</u> way to spot one is to ask yourself if it tells you about the <u>relation</u> between two things. If it <u>does</u>, then it's a <u>preposition</u>.

Prepositions <u>are about</u> Time <u>as well as</u> Place

Prepositions can tell you about <u>when</u> things are as well as <u>where</u> they are.

Let's go for a coffee <u>after</u> work.

Carrie walked the dinosaurs <u>before</u> she did her homework.

Hassan span round and round <u>until</u> he fell over.

Uncomfortable? Get into a better preposition...

<u>Prepositions</u> — another of those dreadful long names for measly little words. There's no point in <u>complaining</u>, you know. They're called prepositions, and that's that. You've just got to <u>learn</u> it.

Sentences — Subject and Verb

You write <u>sentences</u> all the time without thinking about it. There are a few things you need to know about sentences to understand how they work. Read on, and learn...

A <u>Sentence</u> has a verb

Remember, a sentence must have a <u>verb</u>. If it doesn't have a verb, it can't make <u>sense</u> — and that'd be about as much use as a <u>chocolate teapot</u>.

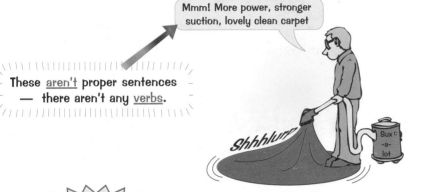

Mmm! More power, stronger suction, lovely clean carpet

These <u>aren't</u> proper sentences — there aren't any <u>verbs</u>.

That's another way of saying it's NO USE AT ALL.

Shhhlurp

The <u>Subject</u> is the Person or Thing <u>Doing</u> the <u>Action</u>

The subject is the person or thing that the sentence is about. The <u>subject</u> and the <u>verb</u> have to <u>agree</u>. This sounds funny, but it really means that a <u>singular</u> subject needs a <u>singular</u> form of the verb, and a <u>plural</u> subject needs a <u>plural</u> form of the verb. Check out this example:

This sentence is <u>about</u> Jay and Andy.

→ Jay and Andy <u>are</u> going to the cinema.

The <u>subject</u> here is 'Jay and Andy', which is <u>plural</u>.

You need a <u>plural</u> form of the verb.

This one's a bit more <u>tricky</u>, so get your brain into <u>top gear</u>, and hold on tight...

This bunch of grapes <u>weighs</u> 240g.

'A bunch of grapes' is singular.

'Weighs' is a singular verb.

You can't write 'A bunch of grapes weigh 240g.' That'd be <u>wrong</u>. The <u>subject</u> of the sentence is 'bunch' <u>not</u> 'grapes'. It's the <u>bunch</u> that weighs 240g.

School — it's like a long prison sentence...

I'm sure you've got to grips with sentence <u>basics</u> by now, but it's time to get down to the <u>nitty gritty</u>. Remember, without a verb it's not a proper sentence. Just make sure you understand that <u>verbs</u> have <u>different forms</u> and they must <u>agree</u> with the <u>subject</u> — it's a doddle really.

Clauses

Look out for <u>clauses</u> — they're just a fancy name for part of a sentence.

A <u>Clause</u> is a bit of a Sentence with a <u>Verb</u>

A <u>clause</u> has a <u>subject</u> and a <u>verb</u>. It <u>isn't</u> a <u>sentence</u>, though, because it doesn't have to start with a <u>capital letter</u> and end with a <u>full stop</u>.

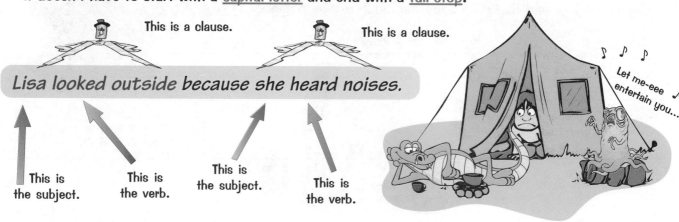

This is a clause.   This is a clause.

Lisa looked outside because she heard noises.

This is the subject.   This is the verb.   This is the subject.   This is the verb.

Let me-eee entertain you...

<u>Compound</u> Sentences have Two Important <u>Clauses</u>

<u>Compound</u> sentences are made of two <u>equally important</u> clauses joined together with a conjunction (a joining word like 'and', 'but' or 'so'). Each clause would make sense on its own as a <u>complete sentence</u> if it had a capital letter and a full stop.

He sat down by the barrel.   Everyone heard him singing.

You can stick these two sentences together with '<u>and</u>' and bingo! You've got yourself a <u>compound sentence</u>.

He sat down by the barrel and everyone heard him singing.

The two <u>clauses</u> in this sentence are just as <u>important</u> as <u>each other</u>.

Important claws? They don't know the half of it.   I think both my claws are pretty important.

<u>Clause</u> — isn't he that jolly fat fellow, ho, ho, ho...

A <u>clause</u> is just part of a sentence which contains its very own <u>verb</u>. If a sentence has two verbs, then it will have two clauses. <u>Compound</u> sentences are really just simple sentences joined together — and that means that both clauses are as <u>important</u> as each other.

Clauses

Hold on to your hats, here's some more really useful information about <u>clauses</u> and <u>sentences</u>.

A <u>Complex</u> Sentence is Built round a <u>Main</u> Clause

<u>Complex</u> sentences are made up of an <u>important</u> clause and some <u>less</u> <u>important</u> clauses. The most important clause is called the <u>main</u> clause.

I'll go on a strict diet when I finish my Easter eggs.

This is the <u>main</u> clause. It is the bit of the sentence that tells you about the <u>main action</u> of the sentence.

The <u>Main Clause</u> Makes Sense on its Own

The <u>most important clause</u> in a complex sentence is called the <u>main clause</u>. The main clause is the one that has the <u>main idea</u> of the sentence. The other clauses are called <u>dependent clauses</u> — because they <u>depend</u> on the main clause to get their meaning.

Fido cycled very quickly after he saw the hotdog van.

This is the <u>main</u> clause. It makes sense on its own

This is a <u>dependent</u> clause. It doesn't make sense on its own.

Harry's Hotdogs

<u>Dependent</u> Clauses add Extra Information

<u>Dependent</u> clauses give you some extra information, but they <u>can't</u> make sense on their own. Another name for dependent clause is <u>subordinate</u> clause.

Natasha laughed until she cried.

This tells you more about Natasha laughing.

Don't give yourself a complex about it...

The difference between <u>compound</u> sentences and <u>complex</u> sentences is a touch difficult to get the hang of. The really important <u>point</u> here is that <u>only one</u> of the bits of a complex sentence would make <u>sense</u> on its <u>own</u> — and that bit's your <u>main clause</u>.

Connectives

Connectives are the <u>words</u> and <u>phrases</u> that connect the different parts of a text.

Connectives join bits of Text Together

<u>Connectives</u> are the glue that holds a text together. They join <u>clauses</u> together in a sentence, and they join <u>sentences</u> together in a long piece of writing. Connectives don't have to be just one word. They can be <u>phrases</u>, like 'in other words' or 'just after that'.

one bit of the text   connective   another bit of the text

Connectives join Clauses in a Sentence

As well as joining words together, <u>connectives</u> join <u>clauses</u> together in a <u>sentence</u>. Some connectives join two clauses that are just as important as each other to make a <u>compound</u> sentence. Some connectives join a <u>dependent</u> clause onto a <u>main</u> clause.

Kenny was hungry, so he ate his own belly.

Here's one clause.

Here's the <u>connective</u> joining them together.

Here's another clause.

Here's the <u>main</u> clause.

I was late because I missed the bus.

This is the <u>dependent</u> clause.

Connectives can Join Sentences in a Text

Connectives show how an <u>argument</u> goes by linking <u>sentences</u> together. You'll see this a lot in <u>discussion</u> articles in newspapers and in <u>letters</u> to newspapers.

The plans for the town square gardens will certainly bring more tourists to the town. <u>On the other hand</u>, it may be several months before building work is completed. <u>Furthermore</u>, the cost to the council, and to taxpayers, is likely to be great.

'On the other hand' brings in a different point of view.

'Furthermore' adds to this point of view.

The commas here are a bit like brackets. See P. 15 for how they work.

Connectives

Lots of words can be connectives — read on and see for yourself.

Several Word Classes can be Connectives

1) Connectives can be Conjunctions

Conjunctions are words that join other words together.

These are conjunctions.

> because, and, but, therefore, also

> Adrian popped his head out <u>because</u> he thought he could hear something.

2) Connectives can be Adverbs

Connective adverbs can be single words or adverb phrases.

These are all adverbs.

> finally, suddenly, surely

These are adverb phrases.

> at last, without stopping, as soon as possible

> The fuse was lit. <u>Suddenly</u>, Dana had second thoughts.

3) Connectives can be Preposition phrases

Connectives like this show the relationship between one sentence and the next. Prepositions are relationship words.

These are prepositions.

> <u>in</u> other words, <u>on</u> the other hand

> Wally wasn't sure where the exit was. <u>In other words</u>, he was lost.

It pays to be well connected...

This is quite a big topic to get your head round, I'm afraid. Connectives do so many different jobs in a text — and, to make matters worse, lots of different kinds of words and phrases can be connectives. The trick is to remember what their basic job is so you'll be able to recognise them.

Punctuating Sentences

Punctuation <u>isn't</u> as hard as it seems. Take a bit of time to <u>learn</u> about full stops and question marks, and you'll <u>never</u> forget them again.

A <u>Full Stop</u> marks the End of a Sentence

<u>Full stops</u> show where one sentence <u>ends</u> and another <u>begins</u>.

Full stop.

Sam put the parcel up to his ear and shook it gently. It rattled.

A <u>Question Mark</u> marks the End of a Question

<u>Question marks</u> go at the end of <u>questions</u>.
A question mark is the <u>same</u> type of punctuation
as a <u>full stop</u>, so <u>don't</u> put a full stop as well.

What time is it?   Question mark.

Watch out! Question marks are only for sentences that actually <u>ask</u> a question. <u>Don't</u> put them at the end of sentences that just tell you <u>about</u> a question.

She asked what time it was.   There's no question mark here.

An <u>Exclamation Mark</u> marks a Strong Sentence

<u>Exclamation</u> marks replace full stops in sentences which show <u>strong feelings</u>.
They are used in sentences to show <u>surprise</u> or <u>fear</u>.

Heave-ho!

They can also be used to show
when people are <u>shouting</u>.

<u>Mark my words</u> — no marks means bad marks...

Full stops, question marks and exclamation marks all show when one sentence <u>stops</u> and another <u>starts</u>, and they tell you <u>what kind</u> of sentence it is. Use a question mark if it's a question and an exclamation mark to show strong feelings. Don't get carried away — too many look awful!!!!!!

Commas

You often need to use a <u>comma</u> to make the <u>meaning</u> of a sentence clear. Commas <u>divide</u> the <u>different bits</u> of a sentence, and let you know that there's a new bit coming.

Commas make the Meaning more Clear

Sentences can be confusing if they don't have the <u>commas</u> in the right places. Take a look at this sentence:

> *Standing beside the giant Lucy looked very small.*

It <u>doesn't</u> make a lot of sense and it makes you think that <u>Lucy was a giant</u>. But if we <u>add</u> a comma:

> *Standing beside the giant, Lucy looked very small.*

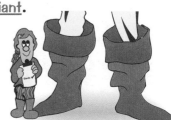

> The comma makes the meaning more clear.

Commas separate Clauses

<u>Commas</u> separate <u>main</u> clauses from <u>dependent</u> clauses in a complex sentence.

> 'When the storm was over' is a <u>dependent clause</u>. It <u>does not</u> make sense as a sentence on its own.

> This is the <u>main clause</u> in the sentence. If you took away the other clause, this would <u>still</u> make sense.

> *When the storm was over, Rob and Becky went home.*

> There's a comma here to separate the two clauses.

<u>Without</u> the comma, the sentence would start 'When the storm was over Rob and Becky...', which gives you the <u>wrong idea</u>. It makes you think of a storm <u>right over their heads</u>, rather than that a storm that had <u>finished</u>.

Comma — no, not a deep sleep...

Commas seem a little bit confusing, but they're there to make things <u>easier</u> for the reader. When you write, think carefully about the boundaries between the <u>different</u> parts of your sentence. You need to put commas in to make the <u>meaning clear</u> to whoever's reading it.

Colons and Semicolons

Colons and semicolons are two more ways to help write sentences which make sense.

Colons introduce Lists

The colon is there to let you know that the list is about to begin.

> You will need the following ingredients: a large ripe mango, 250g of strawberries, 2tsp of brown sugar, 50g of grated coconut and a skinny man with an umbrella.

Colons introduce an Explanation

Colons are used to divide a sentence where the second part explains the first part, or tells you a lot more about it.

> The office was empty: everyone had finished work and gone home.

Semicolons divide Clauses in a Sentence

Semicolons are used to turn two sentences into one. The two sentences must be about the same thing, and they must be of equal importance to one another.

> The door creaked open; the little Creep tiptoed shyly into the room.

Semicolons break up Lists

Semicolons are used to break up lists when the items in the list are long phrases or clauses. If the items in the list have got their own punctuation, you definitely need to use a semicolon.

> At the fête there were stalls selling cakes; a 'guess the weight of the cow' competition; children dancing round a maypole; and a swimming pool filled with orangeade, in which the children were splashing around.

Colons — I have a gut feeling about them...

The difference between colons and semicolons needs a bit of hard thought. Colons introduce something like a list or an explanation, and semicolons are like a stronger version of the comma.

15

Brackets

Brackets, commas and dashes can all be used to separate an extra piece of information from the main body of the sentence.

Brackets separate text from the Main Sentence

Brackets are used to bring something extra into a sentence. The extra something can be an explanation, an interruption, or something that occurred to the narrator as an afterthought. Brackets are always used in pairs. They go around the extra words to keep them separate.

Jed and Ted (the twins) have just learnt jujitsu.

This information interrupts the sentence.

Dashes and Commas can be used like Brackets

You can use commas like brackets to separate off extra information in a sentence.

'Stilton is the finest cheese in the world' is the main clause.

Stilton is, I believe, the finest cheese in the world.

Dashes can be used instead of brackets. You don't always have to use dashes in pairs. You can use a single dash to mark a pause in the sentence or to show where a list is about to begin.

Justin took his two ferrets — their names were Derek and Clive — for a walk.

This part of the sentence gives you extra information about the ferrets.

I peered into the shed and there on a shelf was — Mary's old violin.

The dash shows a dramatic pause.

I like all kinds of fish — cod, haddock, plaice, goldfish.

The dash marks the start of a list.

Nice fishy...

Use commas for brackets — your shelves'll fall down...

Putting things in brackets is easy enough to get the hang of. The only problem is that you might forget the second bracket if you weren't 100% awake — and that would be a bit of a disaster. You can use commas and dashes like brackets, too. This book often uses a dash for a pause.

16

Speech Marks

Speech marks are used around words that someone has <u>spoken</u>.

<u>Direct</u> speech uses Speech Marks

Direct speech is when someone's actually talking. Speech marks go <u>before</u> and <u>after</u> the <u>spoken words</u>. You must always use a <u>capital letter</u> when someone <u>starts</u> to <u>speak</u>.

<u>Capital letter</u> here.
Someone has <u>started</u>
to speak.

Tony said, "We're going on holiday next week."

The <u>comma</u> goes before
the speech marks.

<u>Full stop</u> here, because the
whole <u>sentence</u> is <u>finished</u>.

"We're going on holiday next week," said Tony.

This <u>comma</u> shows that the
<u>sentence</u> isn't <u>finished</u>.

"Do you think," he asked, "that I should take my pogo stick with me?"

This comma lets you know that the
speech is about to <u>start again</u>.

<u>No</u> capital letter here. The sentence
is <u>carrying on</u> from before.

<u>Reported</u> speech doesn't use Speech Marks

Writing <u>about</u> what someone has said in your <u>own words</u> is called <u>reported speech</u>. <u>Don't</u> use <u>speech marks</u> for reported speech, they are only used to show the <u>exact words</u> spoken.

This is direct speech.

Angus said, "I hate sweetcorn."

This verb is in the
present tense.

This is reported speech.

Angus said that he hated sweetcorn.

There are no speech marks.

It's 'hated', not 'hate' here.
The verb is in the past tense now.

Speech marks — the Queen gets 10 out of 10...

Working out where to put things like <u>commas</u> and <u>full stops</u> with <u>speech marks</u> isn't the easiest thing ever, I admit, but if you learn this stuff you needn't ever get it wrong. Remember these tips for <u>reported speech</u>: don't use speech marks, and remember to put the verb in the <u>past tense</u>.

SECTION THREE — PUNCTUATION

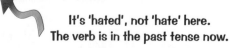

Bullets and Asterisks

Bullet points and asterisks are used to help you look in the right places when you're reading.

Bullet points show where a New Point Starts

Bullet points are dots put at the beginning of a paragraph or body of text to help you see where each new point begins.

You can see at a glance that there are four main points here.

Salworth Park has so much to offer!

- *8000m² boating lake with separate areas for swimming, rowing and windsurfing.*
- *Children's petting zoo with rare breeds of sheep, ducks, rabbits and many more.*
- *Roller coaster rides in our Amusement Park.*
- *Licensed Restaurant, two snack bars and an authentic Italian ice cream parlour.*

Asterisks draw your Attention to a Point

An asterisk is a star shaped punctuation mark that's used to draw the reader's attention to something important. It's used in two ways that you need to know about.

1) Asterisks are used as fancy bullet points.

I don't see what is so fancy about that.

There's an asterisk at the start of each main point.

We must all promise to:
* keep the house tidy.
* do the washing up every day.

2) Asterisks are used to point you to a footnote. This can be to explain a difficult word in the text.

Upon his retirement, Mr Johnson sequestered* himself from the world in a cottage in the Scottish Highlands.

*sequester: to put apart, to isolate .

You see the asterisk here...

...and then you find it again here.

Bang! — now I have your attention...

Not the hardest thing in the world, this. Bullet points show where each new point begins. Asterisks can be used for the same thing or to highlight words which have a footnote to explain them later.

Apostrophes

Even if you've already studied <u>apostrophes</u>, it's time to check you understand them <u>again</u>.

Apostrophes show that Something Belongs

To show that something <u>belongs</u> to someone, use an <u>apostrophe</u> and an '<u>s</u>' after their name.

> Mary's caterpillars are mostly orange and furry.

If the person's name <u>already</u> ends in an '<u>s</u>', you can either add an <u>apostrophe</u> and <u>another</u> 's', or you can just add an <u>apostrophe</u>.

Marcus's toffees have stuck together.

Apostrophe and 's' here.

> Yiannis' toaster is broken.

There's just an apostrophe this time.

> Jesus' parables taught people about right and wrong.

Jesus' never has another 's', only an apostrophe.

For Groups of People...

When you're writing about a <u>group</u> of people or things that ends in 's', you only need to add an <u>apostrophe</u>. <u>Don't</u> put another 's'.

> The witches' hats all need dry-cleaning.

When you're writing about a <u>group</u> of people or things that <u>doesn't</u> end in 's', add an <u>apostrophe</u> and '<u>s</u>'.

> I'm looking for a shop that sells children's shoes.

Apostrophe — a trophy that comes by post...

It's easy to get this stuff really. You use apostrophe "s" unless it's a <u>plural</u> that ends in "s". There are a few pesky <u>exceptions</u> that you're just gonna have to learn, but that's life.

Word Sounds

Well, here are <u>two</u> long <u>complicated</u> words to start you off in this section.
The good news is that you should have met both of them <u>before</u>, and they're both <u>good fun</u>.

Alliteration _is where Consonants are Repeated_

Alliteration gives a nice <u>pattern</u> to a phrase. Some <u>poetry</u> uses a lot of alliteration.
Advertising <u>slogans</u> use alliteration to make you <u>remember</u> the name of th e product.

Sally's slipper slipped on a slimy slug.

You've got lots of 's'-sounds in this sentence.

<u>Tongue twisters</u> use <u>alliteration</u> along with repetition of similar consonant sounds.

Onomatopoeia — _when it Sounds like what it Means_

What a <u>huge</u> long word for something pretty simple. Words like 'fizz',
'buzz', 'crash' and 'crunch' — that's all we're talking about.

Making up your own onomatopoeic
words can be good fun too.

Flip-flops — _onomatopoeia and alliteration for feet..._

Two <u>important</u> words on this page — luckily, they're not too tricky. <u>Alliteration</u> is just repeating
consonants to get a groovy effect. <u>Onomatopoeic</u> words sound like what they're describing.

Imagery

Imagery is brilliant because it makes writing much more lively and interesting.
Imagery helps you to understand by giving you a picture in your head.

Imagery is writing that creates a Picture

Imagery is where language is used to give you a clear and vivid picture, or image, of something.
Imagery brings things in the text to life, and makes you see them in your head.

Her hat was like a bird's nest perched on top of her head.

This makes you see a birds nest in your mind, which gives you an idea of what the hat was like.

Her hat isn't really a birds nest, but you're made to think that it's similar to one.

Figurative writing Isn't meant Literally

The difference between literal and figurative language is something
you pick up without even trying — and probably take for granted.

LITERAL

— it means exactly what it says.

Dave is a real clown.

You don't mean clown as in circus here. It's a way of saying that someone's funny, or that they like playing jokes.

If you're talking about an actual clown called Dave, then that's a literal statement.

FIGURATIVE

— it's giving you a picture.

If you're talking about a boy called Dave who jokes around a lot, then that's a figurative statement.

Vincent van Gogh — he creates pictures...

Imagery is the name for colourful, vivid writing that brings things to life inside your head and makes you see them clearly. Without imagery, reading and writing would be deadly boring, and it'd be much harder to know what a writer wanted you to see or feel when you read a book.

Imagery

You have to know the names of these three kinds of <u>imagery</u>.
The names will take a bit of learning, I'm afraid.

A <u>Simile</u> says that One thing is <u>Like</u> Another

A <u>simile</u> is a way of describing something by <u>comparing</u> it to something else.

> *Fiona looks as miserable <u>as</u> a camel chewing a lemon.*

> Similes always use a <u>comparing</u> word like 'as' or 'like'.

> *His cheeks were pale and saggy, <u>like</u> underdone Yorkshire pudding.*

A <u>Metaphor</u> says that One thing <u>Is</u> Another

A <u>metaphor</u> says that one thing actually is something else.
It isn't meant literally, though. It's a way of creating a vivid
image by making you think of <u>both</u> things at the same time.

> *His eyes were deep black oily pools.*

<u>Personification</u> talks about a Thing like it's a Person

<u>Personification</u> is a special kind of metaphor. It's where you write about
something like the weather as if it's <u>a person</u> with thoughts and feelings.

> *The sun's trying to break through the clouds.*

The sea races up the beach.
He gnaws at the rocks and growls hungrily.

> This talks about the sea as if it's a dog. You can use this sort of personification in poems.

<u>Simile — I thought you said silly me...</u>

Using <u>imagery</u> to conjure up pictures in people's heads is a great way to make writing interesting.
Get the difference between <u>similes</u> and <u>metaphors</u> sorted out in your mind. Don't be put off by that
big word <u>personification</u> — it's just talking about a thing as if it's a <u>person</u>.

Idiom & Cliché

These two new words, idiom and cliché, are about everyday phrases.

Idioms are Phrases that aren't Meant Literally

Idiom is a funny-looking word. Idioms are common little phrases that most people use and understand. The thing is, you can't work out what they mean just by looking at the literal, everyday meaning of the words. You have to know what an idiom means.

under the weather
take the biscuit
keep your hair on

blow hot and cold
wrapped round her little finger

Clichés are overused Phrases

Cliché — another weird-looking word. (You pronounce it 'clee-shay', by the way.) It means a phrase that's been used too much so it's become boring. Clichés are often metaphors.

 At the end of the day. ⬅ Sports people say this a lot, and now everyone says it.

Politicians and business people say this when they mean that things ought to be fair. ➡ *There must be a level playing field.*

It's alright to use clichés when you talk, but it's not a good plan to use them in writing. Use your imagination and think of something original.

Proverbs are phrases that Give Advice

Proverbs work by saying something about nature, or about one part of life. You're meant to extend what they say to life in general.

Too many cooks spoil the broth.

 This means it's a bad idea to have too many people working on a project.

Idiom — can't even spell 'idiot', eh...

These three things are all connected — clichés and proverbs are both types of idiom. Any everyday phrases that don't make much sense are usually idioms.

Acronyms and Mnemonics

These are tricks that <u>shorten</u> words or make them <u>easier</u> to remember. The names are a bit long and scary, but don't let that put you off — just <u>learn</u> them.

<u>Acronyms</u> <u>are made of the First Letters of Words</u>

<u>Acronyms</u> are words made out of the <u>first letter</u> of each word of a phrase.

laser = light amplification by stimulated emission of radiation

I wouldn't want to bother with saying all of this.

CD = compact disc

NATO= North Atlantic Treaty Organisation.

<u>Mnemonics</u> <u>help you Remember Things</u>

This <u>is</u> a difficult word to remember, and it's pretty hard to say, too.
The key to saying it is to keep the 'm' at the front <u>silent</u> — it's just 'Nem-onic'.
<u>Mnemonics</u> are <u>silly sentences</u> you make up to help you remember something.

*Never Eat Soggy Waffles -
North East South West*

The <u>mnemonic</u> needn't always be a silly sentence. It can be something that <u>reminds you</u> of the right way to <u>spell</u> the bit of the word that gives you gyp.

Separate means apart

I Go Home Tonight

<u>Cough cough — a nasty case of mnemonic flu...</u>

<u>Acronyms</u> and <u>mnemonics</u> are fun to make up. Mnemonics help you remember <u>spellings</u> and <u>facts</u> like the order of the planets in the solar system, or anything else you need to learn.

Biography and Autobiography

Biography and autobiography are non-fiction. They're the stories of real people's lives. You could write a biography of someone famous or someone that you know.

Biography is writing about Someone Else's Life

The story of a person's life and achievements written by someone else is called a biography.

Fred Banana was born in Cleethorpes in 1967. His parents were both in the toothpaste trade. He was the youngest of three children, and his childhood was a happy one, full of fun and laughter.

This is Fred Banana's biography.

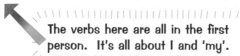

The verbs here are all in the third person. It's all about 'he' and 'his'.

Autobiography is writing about Someone's Own Life

When somebody writes their own life story, it's called an autobiography.

I was born in 1967, in Cleethorpes. I had two older brothers, Brian and Eric. My father, Bert, was a travelling toothpaste salesman, and my mother, Pearl, worked at home making toothpaste out of seashells and soap powder. Those were happy days.

This is Fred Banana's autobiography.

The verbs here are all in the first person. It's all about I and 'my'.

Auto means by itself, or to itself.
Automatic means it works by itself.
Autobiography means writing about your life that you do yourself.

Let me tell you the story of my life...

These two words look rather similar, but don't get them confused. Autobiography is something you write about yourself. If it says 'I was born...' or 'I had...', then it's an autobiography.

CVs and Obituaries

Here are two more kinds of text that tell a life story. They're very different, so make sure you learn what they are and why you write them.

A CV is a List of what You've Done in Your Life

CV stands for Curriculum Vitae, which is Latin for 'the course of your life'.
A CV has a list of school qualifications and all the jobs a person's had. People who are looking for a job give CVs to employers to tell them what experience they have.

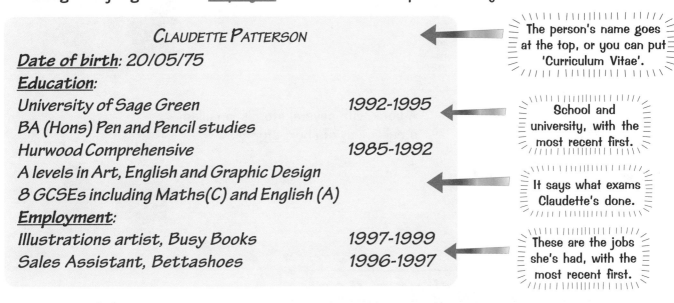

CLAUDETTE PATTERSON
Date of birth: 20/05/75
Education:
University of Sage Green   1992-1995
BA (Hons) Pen and Pencil studies
Hurwood Comprehensive   1985-1992
A levels in Art, English and Graphic Design
8 GCSEs including Maths(C) and English (A)
Employment:
Illustrations artist, Busy Books   1997-1999
Sales Assistant, Bettashoes   1996-1997

The person's name goes at the top, or you can put 'Curriculum Vitae'.

School and university, with the most recent first.

It says what exams Claudette's done.

These are the jobs she's had, with the most recent first.

An Obituary is written about Someone when they Die

An obituary gives a person's life story, and is published when they die.
When someone famous dies, their obituary is published in the newspapers.

Terry Coconut: 1935-1999
Terry Coconut was one of Britain's foremost duck wrestlers. In his prime, he could take on up to nine mallards simultaneously. His death at the age of 64 marks the end of an era for the noble sport of duck wrestling.

The obituary tells you about the person.

It says that they will be missed, or words to that effect.

A fish's life story — that's a 'Sea V'...

There you have it, two more kinds of life story. CVs are really important for getting jobs. They show employers who you are and what you've done so far. You don't need to remember the long Latin words. Obituaries are a way of showing respect for someone who has passed away.

Novels

Here's some stuff for you to learn for when you're writing your first <u>blockbuster</u>.

A <u>Novel</u> is a long story that Fills a Whole Book

A <u>novel</u> is a long fictional story divided up into <u>chapters</u>.
It always takes up a <u>whole book</u>.

No pictures!!!

I love books with lots of lovely pictures.

A book with several stories is called
a <u>collection</u> of <u>short stories</u>.

I like short stories.

A <u>Chapter</u> is part of a Book

A <u>chapter</u> in a novel tells you part of the story. The author often starts a
new chapter when a lot of <u>time</u> has gone by since the last piece of action,
or when he/she wants to talk about different <u>people</u> or a different <u>place</u>.

A chapter in a <u>non-fiction</u> book will give you information on <u>one topic</u>.

That's gross.

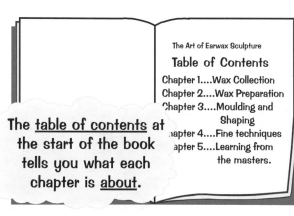

The <u>table of contents</u> at
the start of the book
tells you what each
chapter is <u>about</u>.

The Art of Earwax Sculpture

Table of Contents

Chapter 1....Wax Collection
Chapter 2....Wax Preparation
Chapter 3....Moulding and
Shaping
Chapter 4....Fine techniques
Chapter 5....Learning from
the masters.

The Art of Earwax Sculpture
Chapter Three
Moulding and Shaping

Earwax is a
particularly versatile
sculpture medium.
The limit to its uses
is your imagination.
To achieve the best
results, follow the steps
outlined in this chapter carefully.
First warm the wax gently.
If the warming process is too
rapid the wax loses its flexibility.

My preferred method of warming
is to place the wax, wrapped in
cling film, in my armpit. After
several minutes the wax will be
soft enough to begin moulding.
Next roll the wax between your
hands for 5-10 minutes (fig 1).

Figure 1 Rolling the wax.

Loft conversion — it's a two storey story...

There's nothing too difficult on this page. <u>Novels</u> are long fictional stories which take up a whole
book. In a novel, <u>one</u> story takes up the whole book. The smaller bits that books are broken up
into are called <u>chapters</u>. A book with lots of stories is a short story <u>collection</u>.

Commentary and Anecdote

Watch out — a commentary can be one of <u>several different things</u>.

A <u>Commentary</u> is writing that makes a <u>Comment</u>

A commentary can be a set of notes <u>explaining</u> a difficult text. A <u>difficult</u> poem might come with a <u>commentary</u> that <u>explains</u> what the harder words <u>mean</u> and tells you what the <u>imagery</u> represents.

My heart is like a singing bird
Whose nest is in a watered shoot;
My heart is like an apple tree
Whose boughs are bent with thick-set fruit
My heart is like a rainbow shell
that paddles in a halcyon sea
My heart is gladder than all these
Because my love is come to me

The imagery used in this verse is of joyful and beautiful things in nature. The poet compares her heart to a happy singing bird, to an apple tree thickly covered in apples and to a seashell in a calm sea.

halcyon: calm

A <u>Commentary</u> can <u>Comment</u> on a Subject in the <u>News</u>

Newspaper <u>editorials</u> are a kind of commentary. They tell the readers what the paper thinks, and try to make the readers <u>agree</u> with them. You can write your own commentary on an important issue. It could be presented as a letter to a newspaper, a leaflet...

- *The 1997 Clean Pants Act gives you the legal right to clean undies.*
- *It's the launderette's responsibility to wash your laundry properly.*
- *In 1998, fifteen launderettes and three manufacturers of washing powder were successfully sued under the terms of the Clean Pants Act.*

Leaflets that make a comment often use <u>lists</u> and <u>bullet points</u> to set out all the important points nice and clearly.

An <u>Anecdote</u> is a real-life Funny Story

An anecdote is a little <u>story</u> about something <u>funny</u> that happened. People tell <u>anecdotes</u> about things that have happened to <u>them</u> to make people <u>laugh</u> or to make a <u>point</u>.

Murray Walker — that's what I call commentary...

Basically, a piece of writing that makes a <u>comment</u> is a commentary. Commentary can also mean a load of <u>notes</u> that help you make sense of a <u>tricky book</u> or <u>poem</u>. Anecdotes are funny stories that you tell out loud. Remember, people often tell <u>anecdotes</u> to make some kind of <u>point</u>.

Who's telling the story?

This page is all about <u>who</u>'s telling the story, and what sort of things they <u>see</u> and <u>feel</u>.

The <u>Narrator</u> is the Person <u>Telling</u> the Story

The <u>narrator</u> is the voice <u>telling</u> the story. Narrators can be <u>in</u> the story themselves, or they can be telling the story about <u>someone else</u>.

Don't get the <u>narrator</u> and the <u>author</u> mixed up.
An author is a real person — the narrator is a <u>made-up character</u>.

The <u>narrator</u> of this story is a <u>mouse</u>. You wouldn't be <u>daft</u> enough to think that it was <u>written</u> by a mouse, though.

> *I stood in the gap by the skirting-board and brushed my fur with my paws. I curled my tail around my feet and tried to look cool. I'd never been on a date before, so I didn't know what to expect. Brian had said that we could go out and have raisins for dinner. Raisins — that sounded very posh.*

<u>Point Of View</u> is what the <u>Narrator</u> Sees and Thinks

It's best to explain this one by examples. If the <u>narrator</u> is an <u>old man</u>, the story will be written from the <u>point of view</u> of an <u>old man</u>. The narrator might <u>comment</u> on what happens in the story, and if he does, those comments will <u>sound like</u> a real old man's views.

> *It was Friday afternoon and those dreadful teenagers from the Close were driving up and down in their car, playing some awful excuse for music. I've asked them time and time again to make less noise, but they don't listen. Suddenly their car puttered to a stop. "Good," I thought.*

It says what the <u>old man</u> sees and thinks, <u>not</u> what the teenagers are thinking.

You kids!

The point of view includes the <u>opinions</u> of the narrator.

Land's End — a point with a view...

These two words are important when you're reading a <u>story</u>. Make sure you understand the big <u>difference</u> between the author and the narrator. The <u>narrator</u> is the voice of the book that <u>tells</u> you the story. A story is written from the <u>narrator</u>'s <u>point of view</u>, which sometimes includes <u>opinions</u>.

Planning and Editing

It does sound like a drag, but these two writing tricks make life <u>much easier</u> in the end.

A <u>Plan</u> helps make <u>Writing Better</u>

Good writing always starts with a <u>plan</u>. Making a plan means putting your thoughts in <u>order</u>, so that your writing is lovely and clear, and easy to <u>understand</u>. <u>Always</u> plan it out first.

STORIES

If you're planning a story, you need to decide what's going to happen and in what order.

Work out what's going to happen at the beginning, in the middle, and at the end of your story.

For <u>non-fiction</u>, write down the <u>points</u> you want to make. Then decide how you're going to <u>join</u> them together. Make it <u>clear</u> and easy to understand.

A plan doesn't need to be in <u>proper</u> sentences. You just need to <u>jot down</u> the things you're going to write about.

Editing <u>is</u> Changing <u>your</u> Writing <u>to make it Better</u>

It seems a bit harsh, but even when you've written your story or article out, you're <u>not</u> finished. When you <u>edit</u> stuff, you want to look for <u>spelling</u>, <u>grammar</u> and <u>punctuation</u> mistakes.

Look at the <u>style</u> you've used and make sure it fits with <u>why</u> you're writing and <u>who's</u> going to read it.

<u>Everything</u> you've said has to be good and <u>clear</u> and easy for <u>someone else</u> to <u>understand</u>. <u>Rewrite</u> bits if you need to.

Perfectly clear...

It's <u>no use</u> at all just thinking, "Oh, it's alright, <u>I</u> know what it means."

Plan it — is that like Mercury or Venus...

This stuff is really <u>important</u>, so don't forget it. If you <u>plan</u> your writing <u>first</u>, you won't end up scrawling a mess of words all over the page. Once you've finished, take extra time to <u>check</u> everything. Even the best writers make a few mistakes — this is how to <u>cut them out</u>.

Parentheses, Footnotes and Appendices

There are some <u>odd</u>-looking words on this page.
They're all about giving the reader a bit of <u>extra information</u> on what they're reading.

Parenthesis = Information added into the Text

A <u>parenthesis</u> is an extra snippet of information added into a text and put inside <u>brackets</u>, <u>commas</u> or <u>dashes</u>. It can be an interruption, an explanation or an afterthought.
See P. 15 for more on brackets. The <u>plural</u> of parenthesis is parentheses.

> *John Stone lost two kilos (in weight) last year.*

Footnotes explain and add Information

They're called footnotes because they're at the <u>foot</u> of the page. Footnotes either explain a <u>difficult</u> word in the text, or they give you some interesting <u>extra</u> information that isn't important enough to go in the <u>main</u> part of the text.

foot note...

The little (1) tells you what number to look for at the bottom of the page

Before the automatic cheese mangle (1),cheese was mangled by hand. This took a lot of effort.
1. These were invented in 1957.

Mary Lewis started making cheese at home between August 1958 and March 1959 (2).
2. These dates are uncertain

Here's your footnote.

An Appendix comes at the End

An <u>appendix</u> is added on at the end of a text. It gives extra information that allows you a <u>broader</u> picture of what the text is talking about. For example, an information book about life in Japan might have an appendix with <u>facts</u> about the <u>size</u> and <u>population</u> of Japan, the <u>climate</u>, what things Japan <u>sells</u> to the rest of the world.

It's at the end of the book.

The plural of appendix is appendices.

Appendix
Area: 377 800 square km
Population: 124 million
Climate: Cool in the north with cold winter, warm all year in the south.
Exports: cars, iron, electrical goods.

Footnotes — are they written in footprints...

These three are all about <u>adding</u> extra stuff onto a text. <u>Parentheses</u> are <u>extra bits</u> of information in added <u>into</u> the text itself. <u>Footnotes</u> go at the end of the page to <u>explain</u> and <u>expand</u> on words in the text. The <u>appendix</u> at the end of a book has lots of juicy titbits of <u>information</u> about the book.

Extracts

When you're writing, you'll need to use <u>bits</u> of <u>texts</u> for <u>examples</u>, or to <u>prove</u> something.

An Extract is a Piece out of a Larger Text

An extract is a short <u>bit</u> taken from a <u>text</u>. If you're given an extract of a <u>story</u> to read, it won't start at the beginning, but somewhere in the <u>middle</u>.

beginning bit... blah blah rhubarb rhubarb blah blah...

...suddenly, all the lights went out. Charlie couldn't see a thing. He felt his way very slowly to the door, trying carefully not to knock anything over...

This bit cut out of the <u>middle</u> of the text is an <u>extract</u>.

The rest of the story will be in the same style, because it all fits together.

...blah blah blah rhubarb rhubarb blah...the end.

A Quotation is copied Exactly from a Text

Quotations are a <u>few words</u> taken from a text. Quotations are used to help make a <u>point</u>. When you write about a <u>story</u> or a <u>poem</u>, it's useful to <u>quote</u> from it so that you can show exactly <u>which bit</u> of the text you're talking about.

Quotations go inside <u>speech marks</u> to show that it's a quote and not written in your own words.

Speech inside the quotation is put in <u>single speech marks</u> so it doesn't get confused with where the quotation starts and stops.

" 'What lies over there?' asked the Mole, waving a paw towards a background of woodland that darkly framed the water meadows on one side of the river. 'That? O, that's just the Wild Wood,' said the Rat shortly. 'We don't go there very much, we river-bankers.' "

When you quote, you <u>must</u> copy out the words <u>exactly</u>.

At least it's not as painful as tooth extraction...

Here are <u>two</u> useful ways of taking bits of writing from a text. <u>Extracts</u> are larger chunks taken from texts to give a feel for the whole text. <u>Quotes</u> are smaller bits taken word-for-word from the text to <u>back up</u> or help to <u>explain</u> a point that someone's making.

SECTION SIX — WORDS ABOUT WRITING

Summing Up

Putting things in a <u>nutshell</u>, that's what this page is all about.

A <u>Synopsis</u> tells you what the <u>Story</u> <u>is</u>

<u>Synopsis</u> is a posh word for a <u>summary</u> of a text. A synopsis of a <u>story</u> tells you the main events of the story in a <u>shortened</u> form. It doesn't include any of the speech or descriptions, and just gives you the <u>bare bones</u> of what happens.

> ### Abdication Street: Chapter Twenty-One
> Fiona confronted Craig about the missing money. Craig pointed the finger at Laura. Duncan overheard Brian and Tina talking about their plans for the corner shop. Jane invited Matthew for dinner.

It just tells you the <u>plot</u>, and nothing else. There aren't any descriptions, and there's <u>no direct speech</u>.

If you missed an episode of a soap opera, you could read a synopsis in a <u>paper</u> or <u>TV guide</u> to find out what happened.

<u>Blurb</u> tells you what a <u>Book</u> <u>is</u> Like

The <u>blurb</u> on the back of a novel has a <u>synopsis</u> of the story so you know what kind of book it's going to be. The blurb <u>won't</u> give away the <u>ending</u>, though. Blurb is always upbeat and <u>positive</u> to make you <u>want</u> to read the book.

A <u>Review</u> says whether you <u>Liked</u> Something

<u>Reviews</u> are written about books, records, restaurants and plays so that people can <u>find out</u> what they're <u>like</u>. A review needs to contain some <u>information</u> about the thing as well as saying whether it was <u>good</u> or <u>bad</u>, and <u>why</u>.

> *Pop Go the Weasels(PG)* A charming animated film about a group of animals who enter the Eurovision Song Contest. Catchy tunes, a gripping storyline, a dash of romance and top-notch performances from Richard E Loan as the band's manager and Denise Campervan-Outing as Wendy Weasel make this a film well worth seeing.

Blurb synopsis — isn't he from Star Wars...

Here are <u>three</u> top ways to find out about a story or film <u>beforehand</u>. They are all slightly different so make sure you understand about <u>each one</u> what information you can get from them.

Styles of Writing

Here are two different <u>styles</u> used in <u>writing</u> that you should know about.

Journalistic *style is used in* Newspaper Articles

<u>Journalists</u> write about the kind of things that their readers will be <u>interested</u> in.
Newspapers write about the <u>same</u> news in <u>different ways</u> to interest <u>different sets</u> of readers.

It was decided yesterday by Parliament to cut housing benefit by just under one third.

Journalistic writing often uses <u>passive</u> verbs.

Marguerite Newsome, MP for Salworth, voted against the savage cuts.

You'll notice <u>clauses</u> and <u>phrases</u> popping in between two commas to give you more information.

Journalists often use <u>emotional</u> and <u>persuasive</u> language to make you side with a particular opinion. They use words like 'outrageous' and 'savage'.

Mother-of-two Jo Stephens, 26, called the cuts outrageous.

NO MORE CUTS!

They like to give people's <u>ages</u>. They do this a lot in <u>tabloid</u> newspapers, like the Sun and the Mirror.

Impersonal *writing is* not *about you, him, her or me*

<u>Impersonal</u> writing talks about groups of people <u>in general</u>, not about individual people like you, me, him or her. It would say 'people' or 'the public' instead of 'us'. Impersonal writing often uses <u>passive</u> verbs so you can't tell exactly who it's talking about.

It just says 'people' — it doesn't say who.

People spend up to 30 hours a week watching television.

It uses the present tense.

<u>Formal</u> writing is usually quite impersonal, and uses the <u>present</u> tense to talk about things that generally happen, or things that keep on happening as a matter of course.

Newspaper style — read all about it...

Next time you're reading a paper have a look at the type of <u>style</u> the writers use. Writers use different styles depending on <u>what kind</u> of article or text they are <u>writing</u> — look out for it.

Parody and Hypothesis

These are two <u>strange</u> looking words — <u>read on</u> to find out their <u>exciting meanings</u>...

A <u>Parody</u> imitates a Text to <u>Make Fun</u> of it

People take the mickey by <u>copying</u> each other, and a <u>parody</u> of a text takes the mickey out of it by imitating it. A parody isn't a straight copy of a text — it goes <u>over the top</u> and <u>exaggerates</u> things to make people laugh, or to show that the original text was a bit silly.

This is a <u>parody</u> of a tabloid story about a <u>celebrity couple</u>.

It uses the <u>same style</u> as a real newspaper, but it <u>exaggerates</u> things by talking about an <u>alien</u>.

United In Love
Footballer to Wed Space Girl

Salworth United star Tony Mulroney announced his engagement yesterday to stunning seven foot tall alien babe, Posh Space.

Out of This World

"It was love at first sight," said Posh Space, real name Zeera, 268. Mulroney, 24, said: "I'm over the moon. She's out of this world."

On Another Planet

Salworth United fanzine editor Ted Drizzle is worried that Posh Space is so used to living on another planet that she won't settle in the area. Downbeat Drizzle, 62, warned: "There's already talk of a £362 million transfer bid for Mulroney from Tharg Rovers".

A <u>Hypothesis</u> is a <u>Theory</u> that isn't Proved

Once again, a word that's difficult to <u>spell</u>, and pretty darned tricky to say, too. If you break it down into chunks, it's <u>easier</u> to say and to remember.

This is a <u>hypothesis</u> until it's tested.

This boat will float on water.

Now he knows that the boat <u>does</u> float on water (but, unfortunately, he doesn't...)

Hypothesis — try saying it with your tongue out...

Two very <u>different</u> kinds of text here. <u>Parodies</u> are good fun — they're all about taking the mickey. If you come up with a <u>hypothesis</u>, you won't be sure it's <u>true</u> until you <u>test</u> it out.

Rhyme

Rhyme is the main trick for making people notice things in poetry.
It's well worth being able to spot it and say something about it.

Words Rhyme if their Endings Sound the Same

Rhyme is used a lot in poetry. It's sometimes hard to tell if two words rhyme just by looking at them. When you read a poem quietly on your own (like in an exam), say it to yourself inside your head so that you don't miss any of the rhymes.

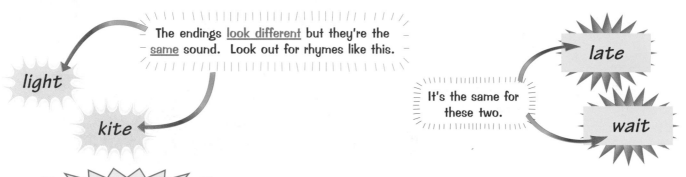

The endings look different but they're the same sound. Look out for rhymes like this.

light

kite

It's the same for these two.

late

wait

Internal Rhyme is in the Middle of a Line

Rhyming words usually come at the end of two lines.
However, you can also have rhymes appearing in the middle of a line.

You try keeping this much hair tidy!

Beware the bear with shaggy hair.

These words all rhyme. It means they really stand out.

He cried out and ran inside to hide.

The internal rhyme helps these words to stand out.

Eeeeeek!

Is it a crime to rhyme all the time?

Rhymes are obvious when you read a poem out loud. Watch out for it whenever you've got to write about poems, because it's one of the main tricks that poets use for effect. Interestingly enough, rhyme can be going on all over the place, not just at the end of each line.

Half-Rhyme and Assonance

Here are some more <u>special poetic effects</u> — make sure you learn this page carefully.

Half-rhyme <u>is when words</u> Almost Rhyme

Some words <u>nearly</u> rhyme — they don't have exactly the same sound, but they are similar, so you say they <u>half-rhyme</u>. Half-rhymes have the <u>same consonants</u> but <u>different vowels</u>. The really fancy name for half-rhyme is <u>consonance</u>.

bun

can

field

build

<u>Half rhyme</u> in <u>poems</u> gives you an effect that isn't as strong as full rhyme. Sometimes it can seem a bit <u>weird</u>, because you almost <u>want</u> it to rhyme exactly and it doesn't.

Assonance <u>is having the Same</u> Vowel Sound

<u>Assonance</u> is when words share the <u>same vowel</u> sound, but the consonants are <u>different</u>.

Last w<u>ee</u>k, L<u>i</u>sa had a p<u>ie</u>ce of ch<u>ee</u>se every night before she went to sl<u>ee</u>p, to help her dr<u>ea</u>m.

All the words in blue have the 'ee' sound in them, but they aren't all spelt with 'ee'.

You wouldn't know it — but I used to be a poet...

All these <u>special effects</u> make my head spin. Half-rhyme and assonance are tough to remember. Just keep this in mind: <u>assonance</u> means the <u>vowels</u> are the <u>same</u> — but the consonants aren't. <u>Half-rhyme</u> means the <u>consonants</u> are the <u>same</u> but the vowels aren't. Make sure you <u>learn</u> that.

Rhythm and Metre

Rhyme isn't the only trick used to make poetry exciting. Poets use rhythm as well.

Rhythm is important in Poetry

A lot of poetry follows a pattern of rhythm. There's a fixed pattern of syllables on each line. If a word has too many syllables, it won't fit with the rest of the line.

Baa, baa black sheep
Have you any wool?
Yes sir, yes sir,
I have a whole warehouse full of wool, cotton, linen and other textiles.

There are far too many syllables here...

A syllable is Stressed if you emphasize it more

po   TA   to

You say this syllable more loudly
when you say the word.

Metre means the Rhythm of a Poem

Metre isn't just a measurement — it's also a name for the rhythm and syllable pattern of a poem.

Some poetry has a pattern of stressed and unstressed syllables.

My mistress' eyes are nothing like the sun.

The pink syllables are the stressed ones.

Had we but world enough, and time.

Be like the gas man — read my metre...

This rhythm and metre business looks harder to get straightened out than good old rhyme. The rhythm of a poem can make all sorts of sound effects, and it can really change the feelings you pick up when you read the piece. There's not an awful lot more to it than that.

Kinds of Poetry

There are lots of <u>different kinds</u> of poetry — make sure you <u>learn</u> these three important types.

Many Songs and Poems are In Rhyming Couplets

If one line <u>rhymes</u> with the <u>next line</u> of a song or poem,
the two lines <u>together</u> form a <u>rhyming couplet</u>.

He reached for the coin that lay deep in the pool,
But could not grasp it: gold made him a fool.

Blank Verse doesn't rhyme but has a metre

Most of <u>Shakespeare's plays</u> contain <u>blank verse</u>.
It's poetry that <u>doesn't rhyme</u> but that usually has a clear <u>metre</u> of <u>ten syllables</u> —
<u>five</u> of them <u>stressed</u> and five unstressed. This metre is called <u>iambic pentameter</u>.

They hand in hand, with wandering steps and slow,
Through Eden took their solitary way.

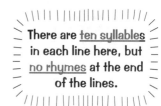

There are <u>ten syllables</u> in each line here, but <u>no rhymes</u> at the end of the lines.

Free Verse doesn't rhyme and doesn't have a metre

<u>Free verse</u> is used by many modern poets, because it's very <u>flexible</u>.
It <u>doesn't</u> use regular <u>rhyme</u> or <u>rhythm</u> patterns.

The end.
It came to me like a curtain
Falling across a stage:
The end.

<u>Don't confuse</u> free verse with blank verse — they <u>aren't</u> the same.

More free verse — I'm not paying for poetry...

These terms may <u>sound</u> tricky, but they're really worth <u>learning</u>. If you can spot <u>rhyming couplets</u>, or notice that a poem is in <u>blank verse</u> or <u>free verse</u>, your essays on poetry will pick up <u>better marks</u>.

Comic Poems

This kind of poetry can be <u>fun</u> — who said all poems are boring...

Limericks are five-line Funny Poems

<u>Limericks</u> are those funny poems that usually start "There was a young man from....."
(Or young woman, or horse, or whatever). There's always a <u>place name</u> in the first line, though.

The <u>rhyme scheme</u> goes like this:
<u>First two</u> lines rhyme, <u>second two</u> lines are different but rhyme together, <u>last</u> line rhymes with the <u>first two</u>.

> When eating fried fish in Nantucket
> You'll find that it's better to suck it
> The flavour seeps through
> Like a jellyfish stew
> Left to rot for five months in a bucket.

Clerihews are four-line Funny Poems

Clerihews are nice, simple little poems. Two <u>rhyming couplets</u>, and that's all — that means that the <u>first two</u> lines <u>rhyme</u> together, and the <u>second two</u> lines <u>rhyme</u> together. They're written to say something <u>funny</u> about somebody, and the <u>first line</u> of the poem is the person's <u>name</u>.

> Gwyneth Dickens
> Has a way with chickens
> There's no need to panic
> If your rooster is manic

Too many Limericks — put a Cork in it then...

Everyone knows a few <u>limericks</u>, they're fun and <u>easy</u> to make up. <u>Clerihew</u> is a strange name but they're <u>straightforward</u> — as long as you don't try to <u>rhyme</u> with a word like orange.

Ballads and Sonnets

You must be able to <u>recognise</u> different kinds of poem, so you'll need to learn a bit about them. This page will help you sort out <u>ballads</u> and <u>sonnets</u>.

Ballads are Poems that tell a Story

<u>Ballads</u> can be <u>poems</u> or <u>songs</u>. They are written to tell a <u>story</u> — often an <u>adventure</u> or a love story. Ballads are usually very <u>long</u> with <u>lots</u> of verses.

The Ballad of the Beast of Howling Moor

It was a cold wet April morn
There upon bleak Howling Moor
A single sparrow sang forlorn
Alone, alone for evermore

A fearsome beast on these hills roams
And none may pass there free from fear
All the peasants fled their homes
When the beast's dread howl grew near

A young man came from the castle gate
His terrible task the beast to slay
His heart grew heavy like a weight
He thought this was his dying day.

At last he stood before the beast
He drew his sword and killed it dead
On that day was song and feast
And many proud "hurrahs" were said.

Ballads are often sung. They were very popular in the past, when few people could read.

This ballad follows a <u>rhyme pattern</u>. Most ballads do, because they're songs.

Sonnets have Fourteen Lines

All sonnets have <u>fourteen lines</u>, and usually follow a clear <u>rhyme pattern</u>. There are several popular patterns — English poets usually use <u>ten-syllable lines</u>.

Ooo, isn't he romantic!

Lots of poets wrote sonnets. <u>Shakespeare</u> wrote some very <u>famous</u> ones, like "Shall I compare thee to a Summer's Day"

Shall I compare thee to a summer's day?
Thou art more lovely and more temperate:
Rough winds do shake the darling buds of May,
And summer's lease hath all too short a date...

Mix them up — get bonnets and salads...

This poetry comes from the dim dark ages before television — a rather <u>scary</u> thought, methinks, but that <u>doesn't</u> mean you can skip it. <u>Sonnets</u> are a bit tricky to write because of the rhyme patterns, but they're fairly easy to <u>recognise</u> because they've <u>always</u> got <u>fourteen</u> lines.

Kennings and Concrete Poetry

These are the last two <u>gems</u> of <u>poetic knowledge</u> in this book. Phew.

Kennings <i>are Descriptions</i>

Kennings are <u>descriptions</u> like 'fly-catcher', 'doughnut-eater', and the like. You can write a poem <u>entirely</u> made up of kennings. Kennings sound very <u>proud</u> and <u>heroic</u>.

RAT SLAYER
ANNIHILATOR OF MICE
DOG CHASER
CHAIR SLEEPER
STAIR SLEEPER
FUR MOUNTAIN
HOUSE LION

Notice how it talks about something and describes it <u>without</u> using its <u>name</u>.

A poem with kennings can have the subject's name in the <u>title</u>, or it can be fun just to <u>guess</u>.

Concrete <i>poems are written in</i> <i>Shapes</i>

You've probably come across <u>concrete poems</u> and shape poems before — now you need to <u>learn</u> the name.

Two titanic tufts
Erupt out of your head.
Like hair fountains.
Like hair waterfalls.
Crazy dancing hair.
Wild leaping hair.
Hair that shimmies
From here to there.

The poem's about <u>bunches</u> and it's written <u>in</u> the bunches on the picture.

Bet you'd never thought of a hairstyle poem...

Sand and cement — pure concrete poetry...

Well, there it is — I bet you never thought <u>poetry</u> could be this exciting. The two new things on this page make for <u>interesting</u> and <u>fun</u> poetry. <u>Concrete poems</u> give all the best bits of <u>drawing</u> and making up <u>poems</u>, so they're pretty much the most fun you can have for free.

Index

Index

Don't forget our other great value Revision Guides —

GCSE English — Writing Skills
EFE4 — £3.50 (£2.00 for Schools)

KS4 English — Grammar
EFG4 — £3.50 (£2.00 for Schools)

GCSE English — Revision Guide
EHR4 — £3.50 (£2.00 for Schools)

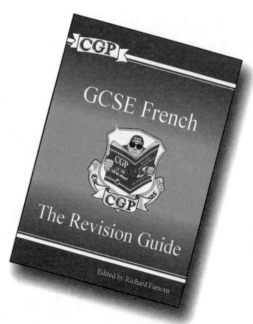

GCSE German Revision Guide
DHR4 — £3.50 (£2.00 for Schools)

GCSE French Revision Guide
FHR4 — £3.50 (£2.00 for Schools)